Harcourt Language

Practice/Reteach Book

Grade 1

Harcourt

Orlando Boston Dallas Chicago San Diego

Visit *The Learning Site!*
www.harcourtschool.com

Printed in the United States of America

ISBN 0-15-320244-0

2 3 4 5 6 7 8 9 10 073 03 02 01

Contents

Name _____

What Are Asking Sentences?

▶ Look at the sentences in the boxes. Write the
asking sentences on the lines.

Are the cookies good?	I pass the cookies.

Is dad's cookie hot?

1. _____

2. _____

▶ Write a new question about the cookies.

3. _____

SCHOOL-HOME CONNECTION
Ask your child to tell how he or she knew that the sentence
in the second box was not an asking sentence.

Unit 1 • Chapter 4
Practice • Asking Sentences

13

Name _____

What Are Asking Sentences?

▶ **Three of these sentences ask a question. Write the asking sentences.**

1. Is that ball mine?

_____

- - - - - - - - - - - - - - - - - - -

_____

2. When will Ted hit?

_____

- - - - - - - - - - - - - - - - - - -

_____

3. Can Max catch it?

_____

- - - - - - - - - - - - - - - - - - -

_____

4. My mitt is new.

_____

- - - - - - - - - - - - - - - - - - -

_____

SCHOOL-HOME CONNECTION
Say a telling sentence. Ask your child
to turn it into an asking sentence.

© Harcourt

Word Order

▶ **Underline each asking sentence that is in order.**

1. Does Matt look at the cat?

2. purr? Can the cat

3. Will the cat meow?

4. Can Matt hug the cat?

5. a pet? Is the cat

▶ **Now turn the other groups of words into asking sentences. Use correct word order.**

6. _____

7. _____

SCHOOL-HOME CONNECTION
Say words that are not in correct word order. Ask your child to say them in correct word order to make an asking sentence.

Unit 1 • Chapter 4
Practice • Asking Sentences 15

© Harcourt

Name _____

Word Order

▶ **Circle the asking sentences in which the words are in order.**

Can Pig pick apples?

Cat like Does apples?

Will Pig and Cat bake the apples?

▶ **Write each asking sentence in order.**

   1. Will Pig a nap? take

     _____

     -

     _____

   2. basket full? Is Pig's

     _____

     -

     _____

SCHOOL-HOME CONNECTION
Say words that are not in order. Ask your child
to say them in order to make an asking sentence.

© Harcourt

Name _____

What Is a Noun?

▶ Draw a line under each word that is a noun.

| girl | clap | duck | dig | lake |

▶ Write a noun to name each picture. Use the words in the box.

| box   doctor   flag   frog |

1.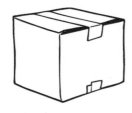

_____

2.

_____

3.

_____

4.

_____

SCHOOL-HOME CONNECTION
Ask your child to write labels to name
five nouns in the kitchen.

Unit 2 • Chapter 6
Practice • Nouns

17

Name _____

What Is a Noun?

▶ **Match the nouns and the pictures.**

1. kite   •   •

2. star   •   •

3. worker   •   •

4. barn   •   •

▶ **Finish each sentence. Use a noun from the top of this page.**

5. Cows sleep in the _____.

6. Matt flew his blue _____.

SCHOOL-HOME CONNECTION
Ask your child to write labels to name
five nouns in his or her room.

© Harcourt

Name _____

Nouns: People and Places

▶ Write a noun for each person or place. Use the words in the boxes.

pond	sister	mom
forest	home	man

1.

_____

- - - - - - - - - - - - - - -

_____

2.

_____

- - - - - - - - - - - - - - -

_____

3.

_____

- - - - - - - - - - - - - - -

_____

4.

_____

- - - - - - - - - - - - - - -

_____

5.

_____

- - - - - - - - - - - - - - -

_____

6.

_____

- - - - - - - - - - - - - - -

_____

SCHOOL-HOME CONNECTION
Ask your child to name some places
he or she would like to visit.

Unit 2 • Chapter 7
Practice • Nouns for People and Places

21

© Harcourt

Name _____

Nouns: People and Places

▶ **Circle the noun that names each person or place. Write the noun.**

1.    man   happy

   _____
   - - - - - - - - - - - - - -
   _____

2.    pond   frog

   _____
   - - - - - - - - - - - - - -
   _____

3.    tall   sister

   _____
   - - - - - - - - - - - - - -
   _____

4.    friend   like

   _____
   - - - - - - - - - - - - - -
   _____

5.    home   big

   _____
   - - - - - - - - - - - - - -
   _____

SCHOOL-HOME CONNECTION
Help your child use both words in a
sentence about each person or place.

© Harcourt

Name _____

Identifying Nouns for People and Places

▶ Trace the ___ 's path from school. Circle the
nouns that name people she sees. Underline
the nouns that name places she sees. Write
each noun in the correct list.

sister   bike shop   friend   home   pond   mom

People   **Places**

_____   _____

_____   _____

_____   _____

_____   _____

_____   _____

SCHOOL-HOME CONNECTION
Talk about the people and places your
child saw on the way home from school.

Unit 2 • Chapter 7
Practice • Nouns for People and Places

23

© Harcourt

Name _____

Identifying Nouns for People and Places

sister   dad   pond   home

▶ **Write the nouns that name a person and a place in each sentence.**

1. My dad likes to go to the pond.

   _____   _____

   - - - - - - - - - - -   - - - - - - - - - - -

   _____   _____

2. My sister has lots of pets at home.

   _____   _____

   - - - - - - - - - - -   - - - - - - - - - - -

   _____   _____

3. My dad built our home.

   _____   _____

   - - - - - - - - - - -   - - - - - - - - - - -

   _____   _____

© Harcourt

SCHOOL-HOME CONNECTION
Ask your child to make up a sentence
about a person and a place.

Name _____

Animals and Things

dog   horse   apple   ball

▶ **Write the noun in each sentence.**

1. My dog is fast. _____

2. Catch the ball! _____

3. I eat an apple. _____

4. The horse is tall. _____

5. One horse ran away. _____

© Harcourt

SCHOOL-HOME CONNECTION
Ask your child to tell whether each
noun names an animal or a thing.

Unit 2 • Chapter 8
Practice • Nouns for Animals and Things

25

Name _____

Animals and Things

▶ Circle the noun that names each animal or thing. Write the noun.

1.  pig
cat

_____
- - - - - - - - - - - - - -
_____

2.  fish
rabbit

_____
- - - - - - - - - - - - - -
_____

3.  clock
ball

_____
- - - - - - - - - - - - - -
_____

4.  fan
apple

_____
- - - - - - - - - - - - - -
_____

5.  dog
robin

_____
- - - - - - - - - - - - - -
_____

6.  eggs
tomato

_____
- - - - - - - - - - - - - -
_____

© Harcourt

SCHOOL-HOME CONNECTION
Ask your child to draw a red line under the animals and a blue line under the things.

Name _____

Identifying Nouns for Animals and Things

▶ Write a noun that names the animal or thing in the picture. Use the words in the boxes.

| fish | hat | map | dog | banjo |

1. Nick has a small _____ .

2. Ellen has two _____ .

3. Ben has a _____ .

4. Kim has a _____ .

5. Dan has a tall _____ .

© Harcourt

SCHOOL-HOME CONNECTION
Ask your child to name other animals
or things to complete each sentence.

Unit 2 • Chapter 8
Practice • Nouns for Animals and Things

27

Name _____

Identifying Nouns for Animals and Things

▶ Write a noun for each animal or thing. Use the
words in the boxes.

duck	tent	mat
box	horse	cat

1.

_____

- - - - - - - - - - - - - - -

_____

2.

_____

- - - - - - - - - - - - - - -

_____

3.

_____

- - - - - - - - - - - - - - -

_____

4.

_____

- - - - - - - - - - - - - - -

_____

5.

_____

- - - - - - - - - - - - - - -

_____

6.

_____

- - - - - - - - - - - - - - -

_____

SCHOOL-HOME CONNECTION
Help your child make a list of nouns
for animals and a list for things.

© Harcourt

Name _____

One and More Than One

▶ **Write the noun that tells about the picture.**

rabbit   rabbits

1. Here is one _____ .

pig   pigs

2. Here are two _____ .

frog   frogs

3. Here are two _____ .

bug   bugs

4. Here is one _____ .

cat   cats

5. Here are two _____ .

SCHOOL-HOME CONNECTION
Ask your child to name things at home,
such as one table, two chairs, five toys.

Name _____

One and More Than One

 duck    ducks

▶ **Write the noun that tells about the picture. Use the words in the boxes.**

apple	bag	egg	hat
apples	bags	eggs	hats

1. _____    _____

2. _____   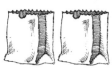 _____

3. _____    _____

4.  _____   _____

SCHOOL-HOME CONNECTION
Write some words that name one thing.
Have your child add *s* and read each word.

© Harcourt

Name _____

Identifying Plural Nouns

▶ **Complete the sentences to tell about the picture. Use the nouns in the boxes.**

ducks	pigs
horse	frogs

_____

1. There is one _____.

2. There are two _____.

3. There are three _____.

4. There are five _____.

© Harcourt

SCHOOL-HOME CONNECTION
Ask your child to use each noun
in another sentence.

Unit 2 • Chapter 9
Practice • Plural Nouns

31

Name _____

Identifying Plural Nouns

▶ **Write the correct noun for each picture. Use the words in the boxes.**

crab	horse	rocks
tree	lamps	hands

1.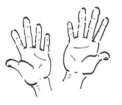

_____
- - - - - - - - - -
_____

2.

_____
- - - - - - - - - -
_____

3.

_____
- - - - - - - - - -
_____

4.

_____
- - - - - - - - - -
_____

5.

_____
- - - - - - - - - -
_____

6.

_____
- - - - - - - - - -
_____

SCHOOL-HOME CONNECTION
Say some nouns, such as *book, flowers, banana*. Ask your child to say the word that names more than one.

© Harcourt

Name _____

Present-Tense Verbs

▶ **Circle the verb in each sentence. Then write the word.**

_____

1. We climb the hill. _____

_____

2. We hike on a path. _____

3. Our dog runs up the hill, too.

_____

_____

4. We rest at the top.

_____

_____

5. We eat our fruit and cake.

_____

_____

SCHOOL-HOME CONNECTION
Ask your child to name some verbs that
tell what she or he did at school today.

© Harcourt

Name _____

Present-Tense Verbs

▶ **Write the verb that completes each sentence.**
  Use the words in the boxes.

hatch	plays	sleeps

walks	eats

_____

1. The chicks _____ from their eggs.

_____

2. Mandy _____ with her dog.

_____

3. Her dad _____ home.

_____

4. The cat _____ on the rug.

_____

5. Her brother _____ a snack.

© Harcourt

SCHOOL-HOME CONNECTION
Ask your child to name some verbs about his
or her favorite activities, such as *play, read, swim*.

Name _____

Adding <u>s</u> to Verbs

▶ **Circle and write the correct verb.**

meet   meets

_____

- - - - - - - - - - - - - - - - -

1. The children _____ at Mike's house.

bring   brings

_____

- - - - - - - - - - - - - - - - -

2. Jane _____ a snack.

walk   walks

_____

- - - - - - - - - - - - - - - - -

3. They _____ to the park.

sees   see

_____

- - - - - - - - - - - - - - - - -

4. Joey _____ a friend.

makes   make

_____

- - - - - - - - - - - - - - - - -

5. The children _____ a kite.

SCHOOL-HOME CONNECTION
Ask your child to explain how the naming
part of each sentence goes with the verb.

Unit 3 • Chapter 11
Practice • Action Verbs
35

Name _____

Adding s to Verbs

▶ **Add s to each verb.
Write the word in
the sentence.**

stand

_____

1. A man _____ .

run

_____

2. A horse _____ .

dance

_____

3. A dog _____ .

clap

_____

4. A little girl _____ .

© Harcourt

SCHOOL-HOME CONNECTION
Have your child read each sentence, substituting
the following words: *men, horses, dogs, little girls.*

Name _____

Am, Is, and Are

▶ Circle <u>am</u>, <u>is</u>, or <u>are</u> to complete each sentence correctly. Then write the word.

is   are

_____

_ _ _ _ _ _ _ _ _ _ _ _ _ _ _ _

1. Today _____ the bike race.

is   am

_____

_ _ _ _ _ _ _ _ _ _ _ _ _ _

2. I _____ ready.

am   are

_____

_ _ _ _ _ _ _ _ _ _ _ _ _ _ _ _

3. All my friends _____ in the race, too.

is   are

_____

_ _ _ _ _ _ _ _ _ _ _ _ _ _ _

4. The race _____ fun.

is   are

_____

_ _ _ _ _ _ _ _ _ _ _ _ _ _ _

5. My mom and dad _____ here.

SCHOOL-HOME CONNECTION
Have your child complete the following
sentences: __ am big. __ is big. __ are big.

Unit 3 • Chapter 12
Practice • The Verbs <u>Am</u>, <u>Is</u>, and <u>Are</u>

37

© Harcourt

Name _____

Am, Is, and Are

I <u>am</u> happy.

Mom <u>is</u> busy.

Pets <u>are</u> fun.

▶ **Write <u>am</u>, <u>is</u>, or <u>are</u> to complete each sentence.**

1. I _____ a girl named Molly.

2. My mother _____ a vet.

3. Five animals _____ in our home now.

4. My dog _____ two years old.

5. Dogs _____ good pets.

SCHOOL-HOME CONNECTION
Ask your child to use *am, is,* and *are*
in sentences.

© Harcourt

Name _____

Using <u>Am</u>, <u>Is</u>, and <u>Are</u>

▶ **Draw a line to match the sentence parts. Then draw a picture to answer the riddle.**

What Am I?

1. I   •   • is outside.

2. Some people •   • is the best weather for me.

3. My home   •   • am a long animal.

4. Hot weather •   • are afraid of me.

_____

- -

What am I? I am a _____.

ǝʞɐus

SCHOOL-HOME CONNECTION
Help your child write a riddle about
another animal, using *am, is,* and *are.*

Unit 3 • Chapter 12
Practice • The Verbs <u>Am</u>, <u>Is</u>, and <u>Are</u>

39

Name _____

Using <u>Am</u>, <u>Is</u>, and <u>Are</u>

▶ **Circle the words that complete the sentence. Color the picture the sentence tells about.**

1. The pigs   **are pink.**

   is pink.

2. The dog   **is hungry.**

   are hungry.

3. The elephants   **is big.**

   are big.

4. I   **am happy.**

   is happy.

▶ **Use <u>is</u> or <u>are</u> to complete the sentence.**

_____

5. The chick _____ small.

SCHOOL-HOME CONNECTION
Ask your child to use *am*, *is*, and *are* at the beginning of questions. Answer the questions.

© Harcourt

Name _____

Past-Tense Verbs

▶ Write the verbs that
   tell about the past.

chirp   chirped

_____

- -

1. The birds _____ all night.

jumped   jump

_____

- -

2. The dog _____ on the bed.

splash   splashed

_____

- -

3. The fish _____ their water.

played   play

_____

- -

4. The cat _____ with her toys.

toss   tossed

_____

- -

5. Carmen _____ in her bed!

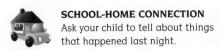

SCHOOL-HOME CONNECTION
Ask your child to tell about things
that happened last night.

Name _____

Past-Tense Verbs

Two goats <u>played</u> in their boat.

They <u>jumped</u> into the water.

▶ **Write the verbs that tell about the past.**

1. The goats painted their
   boat green.

   _____

2. They shouted "Hello!"
   to all their friends.

   _____

3. They added a sail to
   their boat.

   _____

4. They sailed their
   boat on the lake.

   _____

5. They ate fish
   for dinner.

   _____

SCHOOL-HOME CONNECTION
Ask your child to say some sentences
about what he or she did in school.

© Harcourt

Name _____

Adding <u>ed</u> to Verbs

▶ **Add <u>ed</u> to the words in the boxes. Then write the correct word in each sentence.**

fix	paint	call
help	want	

_____

1. Last night I _____ my mother.

_____

2. We _____ Max out of his doghouse.

_____

3. We _____ the walls.

_____

4. We _____ the door.

_____

5. Max _____ to get back in his home!

© Harcourt

SCHOOL-HOME CONNECTION
Ask your child to tell about something you did together in the past.

Unit 3 • Chapter 13
Practice • Past-Tense Verbs

43

Name _____

Adding ed to Verbs

▶ **Underline each verb that tells about the past.**

1. fill   filled   2. picked   pick

3. shouted   shouts   4. want   wanted

5. jumped   jumping   6. roll   rolled

7. walk   walked   8. helped   help

▶ **Add ed to each verb to tell about the past.**

9. look   _____

10. play   _____

11. point   _____

12. chirp   _____

SCHOOL-HOME CONNECTION
Have your child use the written
words in sentences.

© Harcourt

Name _____

Was and Were

▶ **Draw a line to complete each sentence.**

1. The bus •   • were red and pink.

2. The trip •   • was big and yellow.

3. The flowers •   • were hungry.

4. The animals •   • was very tall.

5. The horse •   • was fun.

▶ **Write was or were to complete the sentence.**

_____

- - - - - - - - - - - - - - - - - - -

The children _____ happy.

SCHOOL-HOME CONNECTION
Have your child use *was* and *were* in
sentences with these words: *I, we, cats, school.*

Unit 3 • Chapter 14
Practice • The Verbs <u>Was</u> and <u>Were</u>   45

© Harcourt

Name _____

Was and Were

Our class play <u>was</u> funny.

The animals <u>were</u> silly.

▶ **Write <u>was</u> or <u>were</u> to complete each sentence.**

_____

1. Dan _____ a caterpillar.

2. Some children _____ pigs.

3. Polly _____ a whale.

4. The songs _____ nice.

5. The play _____ very good.

SCHOOL-HOME CONNECTION
Have your child use *was* and *were*
in some sentences.

© Harcourt

Name _____

Using <u>Was</u> and <u>Were</u>

▶ **Write <u>was</u> or <u>were</u> to complete the sentences.**

Dear Gram,

 Last night we went to a play.

_____

The story _____ wonderful.

The people _____ funny.

It _____ a very long play.

We _____ all tired!

 Love,

 Lilly

SCHOOL-HOME CONNECTION
Help your child write a letter to a family
member. Use *was* and *were*.

Unit 3 • Chapter 14
Practice • The Verbs <u>Was</u> and <u>Were</u>
47

© Harcourt

Name _____

Using <u>Was</u> and <u>Were</u>

▶ **Circle <u>was</u> or <u>were</u> to complete each sentence. Write the sentence.**

1. The party ___ fun.   **was**   **were**

   _____

   - - - - - - - - - - - - - - - - - - -

   _____

2. The hats ___ silly.   **was**   **were**

   _____

   - - - - - - - - - - - - - - - - - - -

   _____

3. Dad ___ busy.   **was**   **were**

   _____

   - - - - - - - - - - - - - - - - - - -

   _____

4. The cake ___ yummy.   **was**   **were**

   _____

   - - - - - - - - - - - - - - - - - - -

   _____

▶ **Draw a picture about a party you went to.**

SCHOOL-HOME CONNECTION
Ask your child to use *was* and *were*
to tell about his or her picture.

© Harcourt

Name _____

Describing Words

▶ Write a different color word under each ball.
Then color the balls to match the words.

red	yellow	blue
green	orange	brown

_____   _____   _____

- - - - - - - - -   - - - - - - - - -   - - - - - - - - -

_____   _____   _____

_____   _____   _____

- - - - - - - - -   - - - - - - - - -   - - - - - - - - -

_____   _____   _____

▶ Circle the words that describe size and shape.
Then finish the sentence with a describing word
that tells your favorite color.

_____

- - - - - - - - -

I like balls that are big, round, and _____.

SCHOOL-HOME CONNECTION
Ask your child to use describing words to tell the
size, shape, and color of one object in the room.

Describing Words

Color  **Size**  **Shape**

yellow   big   round

▶ **Answer each question. Write the describing word that tells about color, size, or shape.**

1. What color are the eggs?   **green   white**

_____

- - - - - - - - - - - - - - - -

_____

2. What size is the bug?   **small   big**

_____

- - - - - - - - - - - - - - - -

_____

3. What shape is the block?   **round   square**

_____

- - - - - - - - - - - - - - - -

_____

SCHOOL-HOME CONNECTION
Ask your child to describe the color, size,
and shape of various objects at home.

© Harcourt

Name _____

Color, Size, and Shape

▶ **Write a describing word for each picture.**

round	little	square
big	green	brown

1.

_____

\- \- \- \- \- \- \- \- \- \-

2.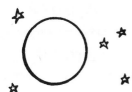

_____

\- \- \- \- \- \- \- \- \- \-

3.

_____

\- \- \- \- \- \- \- \- \- \-

4.

_____

\- \- \- \- \- \- \- \- \- \-

5.

_____

\- \- \- \- \- \- \- \- \- \-

6.

_____

\- \- \- \- \- \- \- \- \- \-

SCHOOL-HOME CONNECTION
Ask your child to think of another
describing word for each picture.

© Harcourt

Color, Size, and Shape

▶ Use the picture and the words in the boxes to complete each sentence.

square	round
small	big

1. The box is _____ .

2. The ball is _____ .

3. The cat is _____ .

4. The dog is _____ .

Unit 4 • Chapter 16
Reteach • Describing Words
for Color, Size, and Shape

SCHOOL-HOME CONNECTION
Ask your child to tell whether each
word describes a color, shape, or a size.

© Harcourt

Name _____

Describing Words for Taste, Smell, Sound and Feel

▶ **Draw a line to match the words in each box with the correct title.**

1.
| loud   quiet |

2.
| cold   hot   bumpy |
| wet   hard |

3.
| salty   sweet   sour |

4.
| sweet   fresh |

• **Taste**

•
Smell

•
Sound

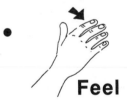
•
Feel

▶ **Choose two of the words to complete this sentence.**

_____   _____

5. Ice cream is _____ and _____.

SCHOOL-HOME CONNECTION
Ask your child to describe how popcorn
tastes, smells, sounds, and feels.

Unit 4 • Chapter 17
Practice • Describing Words for
Taste, Smell, Sound, and Feel
53

Name _____

Describing Words for Taste, Smell, Sound, and Feel

Lemons taste <u>sour</u>.
They feel <u>hard</u>.
They smell <u>fresh</u>.

▶ **Circle the word in each sentence that describes how something tastes, smells, sounds, or feels. Write the word.**

1. The cake tastes sweet.

_____

- - - - - - - - - - - - - -

_____

2. The fruit smells fresh.

_____

- - - - - - - - - - - - - -

_____

3. The horn is so loud!

_____

- - - - - - - - - - - - - -

_____

4. The puppy feels soft.

_____

- - - - - - - - - - - - - -

_____

SCHOOL-HOME CONNECTION
Ask your child to use the describing words to tell about some other things.

© Harcourt

Name _____

More Describing Words

▶ **Use words from the boxes to complete each sentence.**

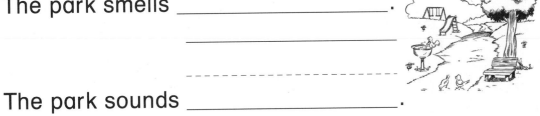

wet	sticky	quiet
sweet	fresh	sour

1. The park smells _____.

   The park sounds _____.

2. The cake tastes _____.

   The cake feels _____.

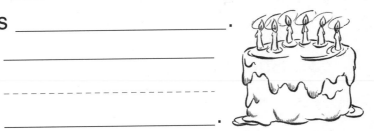

3. The drink feels _____.

   The drink tastes _____.

Name _____

More Describing Words

▶ **Write a describing word from the boxes for each sentence.**

salty	hot	soft

loud	sweet

1. He tastes the _____ snack.

2. She smells the _____ garden.

3. She makes a _____ sound.

4. He pets the _____ kitten.

5. He holds the _____ drink.

SCHOOL-HOME CONNECTION
Ask your child to tell how various objects
at home taste, smell, sound, or feel.

© Harcourt

Name _____

Using Numbers in Sentences

one	two	three	four	five

six	seven	eight	nine	ten

▶ **Write the number word to complete each sentence.**

_____

1. There are _____ fat hippos.

2. There are _____ long snakes.

3. I see _____ kangaroos.

4. I can find _____ tall tiger.

🚒 **SCHOOL-HOME CONNECTION**
Ask your child to write the number word that tells how many bears are in the picture.

© Harcourt

Name _____

Using Numbers in Sentences

one   two   three

▶ **Complete each sentence with a number word. Use the pictures to help you.**

1. Jenny bakes _____ cakes.

2. Mike pets _____ rabbits.

3. Jack reads _____ book.

4. Mom cooks _____ onions.

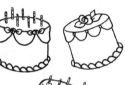

SCHOOL-HOME CONNECTION
Ask your child to use numbers to describe things at home; for example, five chairs, one TV, three windows.

© Harcourt

Name _____

Using Number Words

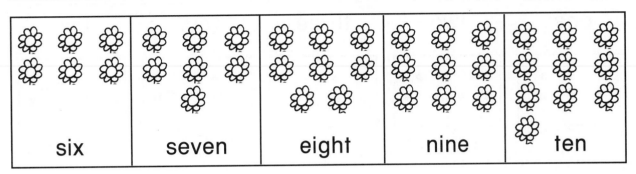

six	seven	eight	nine	ten

▶ **Write a number word to tell how many.**

1. ✏️✏️✏️✏️✏️✏️✏️✏️

_____

- - - - - - - - - - - - - -

_____

2. 🐝🐝🐝🐝🐝

_____

- - - - - - - - - - - - - -

3. 🎩🎩🎩🎩🎩🎩

_____

- - - - - - - - - - - - - -

4. 🐹🐹

_____

- - - - - - - - - - - - - -

5. 🐟🐟🐟🐟🐟🐟🐟🐟🐟🐟

_____

- - - - - - - - - - - - - -

6.

_____

- - - - - - - - - - - - - -

SCHOOL-HOME CONNECTION
Ask your child to draw pictures for the
number words he or she did not write.

Unit 4 • Chapter 18
Practice • Describing Words for Numbers

59

© Harcourt

Name _____

Using Number Words

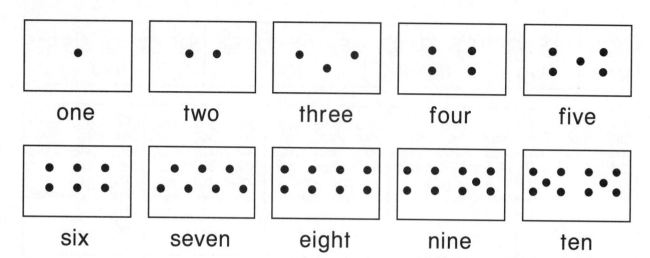

| one | two | three | four | five |

| six | seven | eight | nine | ten |

▶ **Draw a line to match each number word to the correct picture.**

1. one •

2. eight •

3. five •

4. four •

5. three •

6. seven •

SCHOOL-HOME CONNECTION
Ask your child to write the following sentence and
complete it with a number word: *I am __ years old.*

© Harcourt

Words with <u>er</u> and <u>est</u>

▶ Draw three pictures to show how three animals compare in size. Use the words from one box to label your pictures.

small	smaller	smallest

big	bigger	biggest

SCHOOL-HOME CONNECTION
Ask your child to say a sentence about each picture.

Unit 4 • Chapter 19
Practice • Describing Words That Compare

61

Name _____

Words with <u>er</u> and <u>est</u>

▶ **Color the longest pencil.**

 long    longer    longest

▶ **Write <u>long</u>, <u>longer</u>, or <u>longest</u> to complete each sentence.**

1. The snake in the box is

   _____

   - - - - - - - - - - - - - - - - - - -

   _____ .

2. The snake on the plant is

   _____

   - - - - - - - - - - - - - - - - - - -

   _____ .

3. This snake is the

   _____

   - - - - - - - - - - - - - - - - - - -

   _____ of all.

SCHOOL-HOME CONNECTION
Ask your child to use the words *tall*, *taller*, and *tallest* in sentences.

© Harcourt

Name _____

Using <u>er</u> and <u>est</u>

▶ **Circle the word that completes each sentence about the picture. Then write the word.**

smaller   smallest

_____

- -

1. The hen is _____ than the pig.

smaller   smallest

_____

- -

2. The pig is _____ than the horse.

tallest   taller

_____

- -

3. The horse is the _____ of all.

smaller   smallest

_____

- -

4. The bird is the _____ of all.

SCHOOL-HOME CONNECTION
Ask your child use the following words in sentences about herself or himself: *happy, happier, happiest.*

Unit 4 • Chapter 19
Practice • Describing Words That Compare

63

© Harcourt

Name _____

Using <u>er</u> and <u>est</u>

▶ **Draw a line from the word to the correct picture.**

1. fast •

2. faster •

3. fastest •

▶ **Write a word to complete each sentence.**

long	longer	longest

1. The cart is _____.

2. The bus is _____.

3. The train is the _____ of all.

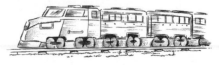

SCHOOL-HOME CONNECTION
Ask your child to use the words *slow*, *slower*, and *slowest* in sentences.

Name _____

More About Days, Months, and Holidays

▶ **Write the name of each holiday correctly.**

1. We visit Gram on thanksgiving day.

_____

- - - - - - - - - - - - - - - - - - -

_____

2. We send cards on valentine's day.

_____

- - - - - - - - - - - - - - - - - - -

_____

3. We see a band on memorial day.

_____

- - - - - - - - - - - - - - - - - - -

_____

4. We put out our flag on flag day.

_____

- - - - - - - - - - - - - - - - - - -

_____

SCHOOL-HOME CONNECTION
Flip through a calendar with your child. Point out
the holidays that occur in the various months.

Name _____

More About Days, Months, and Holidays

▶ **Write the beginning letter for each month.**

☐anuary	☐ebruary	☐arch	☐pril
☐ay	☐une	☐uly	☐ugust
☐eptember	☐ctober	☐ovember	☐ecember

▶ **Write the name of a month in each sentence.**

1. The first month is _____.

2. The last month is _____.

3. I like _____ the best.

SCHOOL-HOME CONNECTION
Discuss why the month named is
your child's favorite month.

© Harcourt

Name _____

Using I and Me

▶ Circle I or me to complete each sentence. Then write the sentence correctly.

1. ___ like pets.   I   me

_____

_____

2. Fish are good pets for ___.   I   me

_____

_____

3. ___ have ten fish now.   I   me

_____

_____

4. Dad helps ___ feed them.   I   me

_____

_____

© Harcourt

SCHOOL-HOME CONNECTION
Ask your child to use the words *I*
and *me* to tell about a pet.

Name _____

Using **I** and **Me**

I had a birthday.

My friends surprised **me**.

▶ **Write I or me to complete each sentence.**

_____

- - - - - - - - - - - - - - - - - - - -

I. _____ am seven today.

_____

- - - - - - - - - - - - - - - - - - - -

2. This box is for _____.

_____

- - - - - - - - - - - - - - - - - - - -

3. Gram gave _____ a pup.

_____

- - - - - - - - - - - - - - - - - - - -

4. _____ call my pup Fred.

_____

- - - - - - - - - - - - - - - - - - - -

5. _____ like Fred a lot.

SCHOOL-HOME CONNECTION
Ask your child to use the words *I*
and *me* in sentences.

© Harcourt

Name _____

I and **Me** in Sentences

▶ **Circle the correct word. Then write it.**

I   me

_____

- - - - - - - - - - - - - - -

1. _____ like to write.

I   me

_____

- - - - - - - - - - - - - - -

2. My big brother helps _____.

I   me

_____

- - - - - - - - - - - - - - -

3. He reads to _____ at night.

I   me

_____

- - - - - - - - - - - - - - -

4. _____ write about animals.

I   me

_____

- - - - - - - - - - - - - - -

5. _____ like horses the best.

SCHOOL-HOME CONNECTION
Help your child write sentences
using the words *I* and *me*.

Unit 5 • Chapter 23
Practice • Using **I** and **Me**

75

© Harcourt

Name _____

I and Me in Sentences

▶ Write **I** or **me**. Color the picture that answers the riddle.

_____

- -

1. _____ float in the sea.

_____

- -

2. _____ can't move on land.

_____

- -

3. You can ride on _____.

What Am I?

SCHOOL-HOME CONNECTION
Help your child write a riddle
using the words **I** and *me*.

© Harcourt

Name _____

He, She, It, and They

▶ What word can take the place of the nouns in each list? Write <u>he</u>, <u>she</u>, <u>it</u>, or <u>they</u> under each cake.

| Ann girl
Gram mom | Jack dad
brother man | boat hippo
cake house | puppies cars
friends eggs |

_____ _____ _____ _____

- - - - - - - - -   - - - - - - - - -   - - - - - - - - -   - - - - - - - - -

_____ _____ _____ _____

▶ Write this sentence using <u>he</u>, <u>she</u>, <u>it</u>, or <u>they</u>.

The birthday cake is very sweet!

_____

- -

_____

SCHOOL-HOME CONNECTION
Say a sentence with one of the words in each cake. Ask your child to repeat the sentence using *he, she, it,* or *they*.

Unit 5 • Chapter 24
Practice • Using <u>He</u>, <u>She</u>, <u>It</u>, and <u>They</u>

77

© Harcourt

Name _____

He, She, It, and They

He made a snack.

They will eat it.

▶ **Write he, she, it, or they to complete each sentence.**

_____

1. _____ like to bake cakes.

_____

2. Today _____ baked a fruit cake.

_____ _____

3. _____ liked _____!

_____

4. _____ will help clean up.

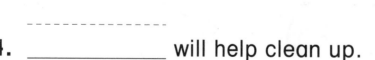

© Harcourt

SCHOOL-HOME CONNECTION
Ask your child to use *he, she, it,*
and *they* in sentences.

Using He, She, It, and They in Sentences

▶ **Write he, she, it, or they to take the place of the noun or nouns in each sentence.**

1. Pam sits in the tent.

   _____

   - - - - - - - - - - - - - - - -

   _____ sits in the tent.

2. The tent has two sides.

   _____

   - - - - - - - - - - - - - - - -

   _____ has two sides.

3. The children are friends.

   _____

   - - - - - - - - - - - - - - - -

   _____ are friends.

4. Tess and Marco think the tent is fun!

   _____

   - - - - - - - - - - - - - - - -

   _____ think the tent is fun!

5. Marco is grinning.

   _____

   - - - - - - - - - - - - - - - -

   _____ is grinning.

SCHOOL-HOME CONNECTION
As you read the page with your child, ask him or her to circle the word or words that *he, she, it,* and *they* refer to.

Unit 5 • Chapter 24
Practice • Using He, She, It, and They

79

© Harcourt

Name _____

Using He, She, It, and They in Sentences

▶ **Write he, she, it, or they to take the place of the underlined word or words in each sentence.**

1. Jenny lost her hippo.

   _____

2. Dad helped Jenny look.

   _____

3. Dad and Jenny looked all day.

   _____

4. Dad found the hippo in a tree.

   _____

5. Jenny was so happy!

   _____

SCHOOL-HOME CONNECTION
Ask your child to explain why she or he wrote *he, she, it,* or *they* for each sentence.

© Harcourt

Name _____

End Punctuation

▶ **Write the sentence from each pair. Circle the punctuation mark at the end of each sentence.**

1. I will sing.   will sing

_____

- -

_____

2. Did you   Did you play tag?

_____

- -

_____

3. Don't kick that can!   Don't

_____

- -

_____

4. The dog   The dog ran.

_____

- -

_____

SCHOOL-HOME CONNECTION
Ask your child to to identify the
end punctuation in each sentence.

© Harcourt

Name _____

End Punctuation

▶ **Write the complete sentences. Then circle the punctuation mark at the end of each sentence.**

_____

1. _____

_____

2. _____

_____

3. _____

SCHOOL-HOME CONNECTION
Discuss the end marks. Then have your child
read the sentences aloud with expression.

© Harcourt

Name _____

Adding End Punctuation

▶ **Read the naming part and the telling part. Then join the parts to write a complete sentence. Write the sentences correctly.**

.
!
?

1. the cat   is surprised

_____

- -

_____

2. is the bug   in the sand

_____

- -

_____

3. Jane   walked home

_____

- -

_____

4. Ducks   play in the grass

_____

- -

_____

SCHOOL-HOME CONNECTION
Ask your child to find a period, a question mark, and an exclamation mark in a book or newspaper.

Unit 6 • Chapter 26
Practice • Punctuation   **83**

Name _____

Adding End Punctuation

The rabbit hopped home.

He was hot!

Are you hungry?

▶ **Write the sentences correctly. Add a** ., **?, or** ! **to the end of each sentence.**

1. the rabbit has an apple

   _____

   -

   _____

   -

   _____

2. it is really big

   _____

   -

   _____

3. is the rabbit happy

   _____

   -

   _____

SCHOOL-HOME CONNECTION
Say some sentences. Ask your child to
identify the correct end punctuation.

© Harcourt

Name _____

Beginning Sentences

▶ **Circle each sentence that is written correctly.**

1. we plan a party.

2. It will be a surprise!

3. i hope nobody tells Liz.

4. We bake a cake.

5. we hide and wait.

▶ **Now write each incorrect sentence correctly.**

6. _____

_____

7. _____

_____

_____

8. _____

SCHOOL-HOME CONNECTION
Ask your child to write sentences to tell what happens next.
Remind your child to capitalize the beginning of sentences.

Unit 6 • Chapter 27
Practice • Capitalization

85

Name _____

Beginning Sentences

▶ **Circle the sentence that uses correct capitalization. Write the sentence on the line.**

1. Mom cooks dinner.   mom cooks dinner.

_____

- -

_____

2. i help my mom.   I help my mom.

_____

- -

_____

3. We make soup.   we make soup.

_____

- -

_____

4. The meal tastes great!   the meal tastes great!

_____

- -

_____

SCHOOL-HOME CONNECTION
Help your child write sentences that tell about a time he or she helped someone. Make sure the first word of each sentence is capitalized.

© Harcourt

Name _____

Correcting Capitalization

▶ **Mark each letter that should be capitalized with ≡. Write the sentence correctly on the line.**

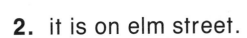

1. matt and jen go to the pond.

_____

- -

_____

_____

- -

_____

2. it is on elm street.

_____

- -

_____

3. they see tadpoles.

_____

- -

_____

SCHOOL-HOME CONNECTION
Ask your child to write sentences about a special place.
Remind your child to capitalize the beginning of
sentences, special names, and the pronoun *I*.

Unit 6 • Chapter 27
Practice • Capitalization

87

© Harcourt

Name _____

Correcting Capitalization

▶ **Mark each letter that should be capitalized with ≡ . Write each letter correctly on the line.**

1. Who is my friend fred?   _____

2. read to find out!   _____

3. He lives in oak Pond.   _____

4. green is his favorite color.   _____

▶ **Use the letters you wrote to spell what Fred is. Draw a picture of Fred.**

_____

_____

SCHOOL-HOME CONNECTION
Ask your child to write sentences about Fred. Remind your child to capitalize the beginning of sentences, special names, and the pronoun I.

© Harcourt

Name _____

Homophones

▶ **Circle the word that best fits each sentence.**
  Write it on the line.

see   sea

_____

- - - - - - - - - - - - - - - - - - - -

1. I _____ a ship.

        see   sea

        _____

        - - - - - - - - - - - - - - - - - - -

2. The ship is on the _____.

        sale   sail

        _____

        - - - - - - - - - - - - - - - - - - -

3. This ship has a _____.

read   red

_____

- - - - - - - - - - - - - - - - - - - -

4. I _____ a book about ships.

SCHOOL-HOME CONNECTION
Ask your child to use each
uncircled word in a sentence.

Unit 6 • Chapter 29
Practice • Troublesome Words

89

© Harcourt

Name _____

Homophones

| sea | see | sail | sale |

▶ **Underline the word that best completes each sentence.**

I. The clothes are on (sail, sale).

2. I (see, sea) a toy boat.

3. The boat has a yellow (sail, sale).

4. I will float it on the (see, sea).

▶ **Draw a picture for the underlined word in each sentence.**

5. Wind blows the sail.   6. The sea is blue.

Name _____

Words That Sound Alike

▶ **Write to, too, or two to complete each sentence.**

_____

1. I go _____ my friend's house.

_____

2. We build _____ snowmen.

_____

3. I like making snowballs, _____ .

_____

4. We sled _____ the bottom.

_____

5. It snowed _____ days in a row.

SCHOOL-HOME CONNECTION
Help your child write sentences using
the words *to, too,* and *two.*

Unit 6 • Chapter 28
Practice • Troublesome Words

91

© Harcourt

Name _____

Words That Sound Alike

I go <u>to</u> the zoo.

My friend goes, <u>too</u>.

We see <u>two</u> elephants.

▶ **Circle the word that belongs in each sentence.**

1. (To, Too, Two) monkeys are playing.

2. They jump from tree (to, too, two) tree.

3. A baby monkey is playing, (to, too, two).

4. It jumps (to, too, two) a branch.

5. The branch is (to, too, two) high.

▶ **Write a sentence using the word <u>two</u>.**

_____

- -

_____

- -

_____

SCHOOL-HOME CONNECTION
Ask your child to tell why she or he
chose *to*, *too*, or *two* for each sentence.

© Harcourt

Name _____

Using Multiple-Meaning Words

▶ **Write a word from the box to name each picture. Use each word two times.**

| bat | bark | ring | row |

1.  _____

2. _____

3. _____

4. _____

5. _____

6. _____

7.  _____

8.  _____

SCHOOL-HOME CONNECTION
Have your child write two sentences using
a word from above two different ways.

Unit 6 • Chapter 29
Practice • More Troublesome Words

93

Name _____

Using Multiple-Meaning Words

 Dad looks at his **watch**.

 We **watch** the horses.

▶ **Draw a line to the picture that matches the underlined word in each sentence.**

1. I hit a ball with my <u>bat</u>. •

2. Rex and Max <u>bark</u>. •

3. I saw a <u>bat</u> fly by. •

4. The oak tree has thick <u>bark</u>. • •

▶ **Write a sentence using one of the words above.**

_____

_ _

_____

SCHOOL-HOME CONNECTION
Invite your child to draw a picture
for his or her sentence.

© Harcourt

Name _____

Different Meanings

▶ **Write a word from the box that fits each sentence pair.**

duck	fall	light	saw

1. Winter comes after ___.

   Leaves ___ from trees.

   _____

2. My bag is ___.

   Use a ___ after dark.

   _____

3. The ___ quacks.

   We ___ in the bushes.

   _____

4. Use a ___ to cut wood.

   We ___ a deer run by.

   _____

SCHOOL-HOME CONNECTION
Challenge your child to write another
sentence pair using a word from the box.

Unit 6 • Chapter 29
Practice • More Troublesome Words

95

© Harcourt

Name _____

Different Meanings

A **fly** buzzes past me.   I wish I could **fly**.

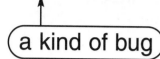
a kind of bug

move through the air

▶ **Circle the word in each sentence pair that has different meanings. Write the word on the line.**

1. We go to the fair.

   The weather is fair.

2. I give the man a dollar bill.
   I win the bird with a big bill.

3. We climb to the top.
   The ride spins like a top.

4. Dad will ring the big bell.
   He wins a ring for me!

SCHOOL-HOME CONNECTION
Ask your child to use each word
in a sentence.

© Harcourt

Name _____

Story About You

> A **story about you** is one kind of story you can write. In a story about you, you tell about something that you did.

1. **Think about things you have done. Choose one thing to write about.**

2. **Tell your story to someone at home. Ask them to write the sentences for you.**

3. **Color a picture for your story.**

MODEL: STORY ABOUT YOU

First, I went to the block corner. Next, I built a tall wall. Then Jessie helped me make it into a castle. We showed our castle to everyone in our class.

SCHOOL-HOME CONNECTION
Have your child dictate a story about himself or herself. Write the story on page 98.

Unit 1 • Chapter 5
Practice • Shared Writing: Story About Us

97

© Harcourt

Name _____

SCHOOL-HOME CONNECTION
Use this page to record your
child's story. (See page 97.)

Name _____

Sentences of Information

When you draw a picture, you can write about it. Your sentences should answer the questions **Who?** **What?** **Where?** and **When?**

1. **Draw a picture.**

2. **Think about what you want to write.**

3. **Answer the questions Who? What? Where? and When?**

MODEL: SENTENCES OF INFORMATION

I got a new pet today. It is a goldfish. I put a little bit of food in her bowl. She swims to the top and eats it. Fishy is a fun pet!

SCHOOL-HOME CONNECTION
Have your child draw a picture
and write sentences on page 100.

Unit 2 • Chapter 10
Practice • Interactive Writing:
Sentences of Information

99

© Harcourt

Name _____

_____

- -

_____

_____

- -

_____

- -

_____

- -

_____

Unit 2 • Chapter 10
Practice • Interactive Writing:
Sentences of Information

SCHOOL-HOME CONNECTION
Your child can use this page to draw a picture
and write sentences about it. (See page 99.)

© Harcourt

Name _____

How-To Sentences

> **How-to sentences** tell how to do or make something. When you write about how to do something, you tell the steps in order.

1. **Think about things you know how to do. Choose one to write about.**

2. **Write how to do that thing. Tell the steps in the right order.**

3. **Use order words like <u>first</u> and <u>last</u>.**

MODEL: HOW-TO SENTENCES

Here's how to wash a dog. First, fill a tub with soap and water. Next, put the dog in the tub and wash him. Then, rinse the dog off with clean water. Last, use a towel to dry the dog.

SCHOOL-HOME CONNECTION
Have your child use page 102 to write
sentences that tell how to do something.

Unit 3 • Chapter 15
Practice • Writing How-To Sentences   101

© Harcourt

Name _____

_____
- -
_____

_____
- -
_____

_____
- -
_____

_____
- -
_____

_____
- -
_____

_____
- -
_____

© Harcourt

Unit 3 • Chapter 15
Practice • Writing How-To Sentences

SCHOOL-HOME CONNECTION
Your child can use this page to write
how-to sentences. (See page 101.)

Description

When you write a **description**, you tell about something. You use words that tell how the thing looks, sounds, tastes, smells, or feels.

1. **Think about something you have seen.**

2. **Write a description. Tell what the thing was like.**

3. **Use words that tell how it looked, sounded, tasted, smelled, or felt.**

MODEL: DESCRIPTION

The Farm

Our class went to a farm. We saw lots of cows. They were big and gentle. The farmers gave us ice cream they made on the farm. It was cold and sweet and good!

SCHOOL-HOME CONNECTION
Have your child write his or her description on page 104.

Unit 4 • Chapter 20
Practice • Writing a Description
103

© Harcourt

Name _____

_____
- -
_____

_____
- -
_____

_____
- -
_____

_____
- -
_____

_____
- -
_____

SCHOOL-HOME CONNECTION
Your child can use this page to
write a description. (See page 103.)

© Harcourt

Name _____

Friendly Letter

You can write a **friendly letter** to someone you know. In it, you tell something about yourself. A friendly letter has five parts.

1. **Think about things to tell about yourself. Choose one idea.**

2. **Write a letter to your friend.**

3. **Use the five parts that are shown by the arrows.**

MODEL: FRIENDLY LETTER

April 17, 200_ ←

→ Dear Sarah,

Today I had my first soccer game. I tried to kick the ball. I missed two times. Then I kicked the ball really hard. It went into the goal! We lost, but we had fun!

Your friend, ←

Kim ←

© Harcourt

SCHOOL-HOME CONNECTION
Have your child write a letter to a friend. Use page 106.

Unit 5 • Chapter 25
Practice • Writing a Friendly Letter

105

Name_____

Unit 5 • Chapter 25
Practice • Writing a Friendly Letter

SCHOOL-HOME CONNECTION
Your child can use this page to write
a friendly letter. (See page 105.)

Name _____

Story

You can write a **story** about someone or something. A story tells what happens to a person, animal, or thing.

1. **Think of ideas for a story. Choose one to write about.**

2. **Write your story. Tell who it is about and what happens.**

3. **Write a title for your story.**

MODEL: STORY

Sam's New Sled

Sam had a new sled, but there was no snow. He waited and waited. At last, he put his sled away. In the morning Sam had a big surprise. It was snowing!

SCHOOL-HOME CONNECTION
Have your child write his or her story on page 108.

© Harcourt

Name _____

Unit 6 • Chapter 30
Practice • Writing a Story

SCHOOL-HOME CONNECTION
Your child can use this page to
write a story. (See page 107.)

© Harcourt

Skills Index

Action verbs, 33–36
    past-tense, 41–44
Am, 37–40
Are, 37–40
Asking sentences, 13–16

Capital letters
    days, 69–70
    holidays, 71
    I, 73–76, 85–86
    months, 72
    sentences, 1–4, 85–88
    special names for animals, 65–67, 88
    special names for people, 65–67, 87
    special names for places, 65–68, 87–88
    titles of people, 65–67

Days of the week, 69–70
Describing words
    colors, 49–51
    er and est, 61–64
    feel, 53–56
    number, 57–60
    shape, 49–52
    size, 49–52
    smell, 53–56
    sound, 53–56
    taste, 53–56
Description, 103–104

End marks
    exclamation mark, 81–84
    period, 1–4, 9–12, 81–84
    question mark, 13–16, 81–84
er and est, 61–64

Friendly letter, 105–106

Grammar, 1–96

He, 77–80
Holidays, 71
Homophones, 89–92
How-to sentences, 101–102

I, 73–76
Is, 37–40
It, 77–80

Letter
    See Friendly letter

Me, 73–76
Months of the year, 72
Multiple-meaning words, 93–96

© Harcourt

Skills Index

Naming parts of a sentence, 5–8
Nouns
    animals, 25–28
    identifying, 7–20
    one and more than one, 29–32
    people, 21–24
    places, 21–24
    plural nouns, 29–32
    special names for animals, 65–67
    special names for people, 65–67
    special names for places, 65–68
    things, 25–28

Period, 1–4, 9–12, 81–84
Punctuation
    end marks, 1–4, 9–16, 81–84
    in a friendly letter, 105
    of titles of people, 65–67

Question mark, 13–16, 81–84

Sentences
    asking, 13–16
    how-to, 101–102
    identifying, 1–4
    information, sentences of, 99–100
    naming parts, 5–8
    telling, 9–12
    telling parts, 5–8
    word order, 11–12, 15–16
She, 77–80
Story, 107
    about you, 97

Telling parts of a sentence, 5–8
Telling sentences, 9–12
They, 77–80
Titles for people, 65–67
Troublesome words, 89–96
    homophones, 89–92
    multiple-meaning words, 93–96

Usage
    am, is, and are, 37–40
    he, she, it, and they, 77–80
    I and me, 73–76
    was and were, 45–48

Verbs
    action verbs, 33–36
    am, is, and are, 37–40
    past-tense verbs, 41–44
    was and were, 45–48

Was, 45–48
Were, 45–48
Word order in sentences, 11–12, 15–16
Writing forms
    description, 103–104
    friendly letter, 105–106
    how-to sentences, 101–102
    sentences of information, 99–100
    story, 107–108
    story about you, 97–98

© Harcourt